MW00962112

After The Last PR

The virtues of living
a runner's life

Dave Griffin

Judy –
Live with passion !

2010 by
Flying Feet Running Programs, LLC
Westminster, MD 21157
dpgflyingfeet@aol.com

Printed and bound in the United States of America

First Printing 2010

For the runners I coach,

who inspire me every day

and

For TJ

Running is the thread that holds

most of the pieces of my life together.

She holds all the rest.

Table of Contents

Preface

Preface

I'm a runner deep down in the core of my person, and I think I've earned the right to say that. In many respects, the words on these pages have documented the experiences that have made me who I am, not just as a runner, but as a person too. My running and my life are forever intertwined.

I would dare to say that every positive quality I possess has either been formed or strengthened through running. If not for running, I would be but a fraction of who I am today. I know that sounds far reaching and maybe you can't understand, but it is true nonetheless.

And, as much as running has contributed to my success, even more, it has enhanced my well being. That's not something I sought to gain from running, it just happened.

Imagine the sense of accomplishment you might feel by making time in the day to do something good for yourself – something that most people aren't willing to do. Imagine how you might feel if you did that everyday for a week, and then for a month. Imagine if you did that for as long as you could remember. How would that make you feel about yourself?

And on the most difficult days, when it was cold, or

hot, when it was windy and rainy, what if you didn't make excuses? And, when something was pulling your attention elsewhere, and it would be easy to let yourself off the hook, what if you didn't? How would that impact your ability to deal with adversity?

Running has taught me that the relief that comes from taking the easy road is short lived, but that the rewards that come from challenging yourself endure. It's taught me the pleasure of a gift is fleeting, but that satisfaction earned is lasting.

I'm not sure most people understand that. The world is full of short cuts and handouts. Assigning responsibility to someone else is commonplace. And yet, when it comes to your own happiness and contentment, delegating is not an option. You've got to find that for yourself.

Of course, I find joy in many things, like the people I love, but nothing else in my life could ever be as good if I wasn't happy with myself. And, for me, nothing has enhanced my self-worth quite like running has.

This book is about much more than running; it's about valuable lessons that I've learned through running. It's about principles that, when applied consistently, can guide a person toward success.

Life can seem pretty complicated, but it doesn't have to be that way. It can be as simple as taking a step in the right direction, finding a path to run on, and then paying attention to the truth and the wisdom that comes along.

And, whether you run or not, if you think that what I've learned while I was running can help you find your own way, by all means, keep reading.

Introduction

After The Last PR

I ran my last personal record (PR) on April 2, 1989 at the age of 28. From 1982 to '89 I raced various distances, from 5K to the marathon, and in that period I ran all my best times. Back then, running was simple. I ran to race fast, and that was pretty much it.

Since then, I haven't come close to beating any of those PRs. So why, you might wonder, am I still running more than twenty years later?

I could give you simple reasons. Running boosts my confidence. It keeps me fit. I enjoy being around other runners. But the real reason is far more complicated than any of those things.

Each time I run, the unwelcome noise of life quiets. The thick pressure of work subsides. In the simple rhythm of running, I come back to the core of myself.

It's there, at my center, where I remember why I'm here. It's there that I remember what I love. There reside the principles and values that guide me. Life pulls me away from all that. Running moves me back.

I can begin a run faced with a complicated dilemma and finish it with clear vision. Every conflict that's thrown my way is resolved when I remember what's important, and running never fails to remind me what that is.

There's more. Running challenges me. A thousand times, it's confronted me with obstacles I didn't think I'd overcome. It's brought fatigue and weariness, and yet even in the throes of exhaustion, it leaves a small burning ember of strength, always just enough. After so many trials, I've learned that hope is always present if you look hard enough, and hope is a precious thing.

I still remember all my fastest races. I remember the toil in the training, the anticipation of the starting lines and the strategy of competition. I can still feel the exhilaration of those finish lines, knowing I'd surpassed my best yet again and wondering where the next plateau would lead me.

When I was running those races, my single motivation was competition, reaching ever higher levels of success. I'm thankful that I had running to feed my competitive spirit, but even more thankful that my competitive spirit led me to running.

I didn't realize it at the time, but searching for my potential as a runner taught me how to find my potential as a person.

In the process of trying to do my best, I learned how to be my best. Running formed my core values, and my core values shape my life.

I'm much slower than I used to be, but that's okay. It's not as much about speed anymore. There's something more important to me – living virtuously.

When it comes to that, I know I still have some unused potential, but each run seems to move me a little bit closer. And that's why I'm still running, so long after my last PR.

Chapter 1

Faith

Trusting in a Set of Beliefs

I was searching through a stack of my old running photographs looking for a spark of inspiration. There are hundreds of memories and stories hidden there, and they seldom fail to rouse an idea.

The pictures span a period of many years, but most of the races are still fixed in my mind, just as the images are fixed on the paper. There is one from my very first marathon. I don't remember exactly how old I was, but my young face shows the inexperience.

My stride is choppy, weighted down with the pain of distance and discouraged pride. I hadn't prepared well, somehow believing that ability alone would be enough. When reality struck, still many miles from the finish line, all I could do was rely on the mercy of knowing that each step was one closer to the end.

Another picture, taken about seven years after the first one, shows a different posture. There is confidence in my expression, concentration in my eyes. My stride is wide and strong as I pull away from the competitors who had tried desperately to stay on my shoulder.

If you looked through the pictures yourself, you would see a parade of images. In the beginning, a boy finds joy as he discovers himself. Slowly, the years become evident as a seasoned competitor emerges. And then, in more recent photographs, a man still tries to find success doing what he loves.

The pictures seem to tell of a seamless journey, like a life that has followed a well-planned course, but that's not the case. There have been starts and stops. There were moments of choice, sometimes understood and sometimes not, that could have changed everything.

I've been the benefactor of good fortune. Blessed with a touch of ability, I stumbled upon running as I searched for identity in my youth. It was only through trial and error that I ultimately found success, and while I know I fell far short of my potential, it is difficult now to feel anything less than satisfied. Running, after all, has shaped me.

The truth is, though, that something more than luck lies at the center of my story. And while I'll never argue that good fortune has played a part in my success, it seems appropriate to give the credit to something much more meaningful.

Faith is the thread that held the pieces of my running journey together. It gave me hope when I was in the throes of exhaustion. It let me believe in myself when I was on the verge of something great. Faith added meaning to victory and gave purpose to the defeat, and it even provided assurance when, for one reason or another, I had to put running aside for a time.

Faith helps us believe what our simple minds can't comprehend. Without it, greatness can fade to ordinary or worse. But with it, a disjointed journey can become spectacular, just like mine.

♦♦♦

Sometimes, the pace of change startles me, and as I parked the car for a run, I couldn't help but think about the news on the radio. It wasn't long ago that we were hearing words like "stability" and "prosperity" and suddenly there was a crisis to deal with.

In times like these, I need something firm to hold onto. Ever since I can remember, running has provided that. When life has brought me sadness or heartache, hardship or insecurity, running has always given me a foundation of security. On this particular day, I needed just a little something more, so I drove to an old fire trail that I remembered from years ago.

The trail is surrounded by miles of wooded acres, and as my run found a tempo, I tried to recall the things I was about to pass. When I was younger I lived close by, and the trail had been a frequent training route.

Even before then, as a boy, I shared the trail with my grandfather. We would walk until we found the lake and then search for beavers along the shoreline. I passed the spot where we would find trees lying along the pathway, casualties of the beaver's work.

As I ran, the sun danced on the water, and I stopped worrying about the news on the radio, but I began thinking about how much time had passed since I'd last moved past that water. In the years since, I had met my wife, and we had started a family. We worked hard to build a life, make a home and raise our kids. Now, they are nearly adults and on their own personal journeys toward independence.

With several miles behind me, I remembered a place where I used to stop and stretch. I started looking for it as the path turned away, and then back down toward the water.

When I came to the spot I was looking for, I stopped and walked down to the edge. There, a large rock stood against a quiet cove. I climbed onto it and listened to my breathing settle down.

The place was exactly as I remembered it. The full trees formed a barrier on the opposite side of the lake, as if to say, "There's enough beauty right here in front of you. No need to look any further." A breeze rippled the surface, and fish played in the deep water under the rock.

For a few moments, it was like no time had passed at all; I was still twenty years old and seeing it all for the very first time. It felt good to stay there for a while.

There was something different about the run back. I was surrounded by stability; it seemed like the path had been untouched since I left it. Being there helped me realize that, despite the passing years and the events surrounding me, I was mostly unchanged myself, much like the aged trees that I ran past. Something about that restored my faith and made me ready for whatever the news would be on the drive back home.

Just before the run was over, as I was about to turn away from the lake, I saw beavers swimming near the shoreline.

♦♦♦

Scott Absher was taking a familiar run in unfamiliar territory. As he ran on the roads around his home in Maryland, his father lay dying in North Carolina. He was trying to figure out how he and his family could get there to say goodbye.

Nine months before, Scott's dad had become ill unexpectedly. There was a surgery, which later seemed unnecessary, and the procedure led to more serious problems. His father was left hospitalized with a feeding tube, fighting for his life.

As Scott ran through his neighborhood, he thought about the past. He realized that it was his father who had taught him that family comes first and that hard work always pays off. His father was a caring, giving man, and he wasn't afraid to let his children know him as a person.

Scott had been running for seven years before his dad became ill. Running gave him the opportunity to stay fit within the confines of his life. He woke up early while everyone else was still sleeping.

His competitive nature got him started, but as he became a more experienced runner, it was the escape from daily stress that kept him running. And, as he struggled to deal with his father's failing health, that daily tranquility became even more important.

He had traveled to North Carolina regularly, watching his father fight courageously, but the challenges mounted.

As the months passed by, the recurring infections took their toll, and his father needed a ventilator to cling to life.

Through all of that, it was running that helped Scott keep a sense of control. He continued his weekly schedule of running regardless of where he was. It helped him slow the world down, if only briefly, so he could deal with the enduring crisis.

As he turned onto his street to finish his run, he knew that this was the end. The doctors had told him that all hope was gone, and his father was simply waiting for the ventilator to be removed.

When Scott stopped at his driveway, there must have been a part of him that wanted to keep running. He must have felt that as long as he did, he wouldn't have to face what was coming.

When he arrived at the hospital in North Carolina, his dad was alive but unaware that his family was gathered beside him. Within an hour, he passed away.

On the day of the funeral, Scott ran up to the park in the Carolina town where he grew up. Many years ago, his father had been a member of the city council that was responsible for building the park. As he ran there, he felt an overwhelming peace, as if his dad was reassuring him – the suffering is over.

Life is always changing. Sometimes we're ready. Sometimes we're not. Either way, those of us who run understand: there is a firm connection between what we gain through running and what we need in life – a foundation of strength and a pathway to peace. As life returns to normal, Scott still has both.

This essay isn't anything like what I expected it to be. I selected several topics and tried to get started on each one of them. Nothing flowed. I'd get a few sentences out and then – nothing.

All the while, I had been thinking about my daughter's approaching birthday. She was about to turn twenty.

Whenever I remember the day she was born, I think about standing in the hallway of the hospital all by myself. Moments before, we were in the midst of excitement and joy when the monitor told the doctors that her heart rate had dropped dramatically.

Before I realized what was happening, they had rushed my wife into the operating room, leaving me alone. As I stood in that hallway, it was my faith that held me together. Somehow, I trusted that she would be okay.

When a nurse came out of the operating room, she saw me and pulled me inside. I walked in just in time to see the doctor lift my daughter into the world, and a few moments later she was in my arms.

As I walked her toward the hospital nursery, I didn't realize how much she would be like me. Her willful nature and her competitive spirit are mirror images of mine. And, I didn't know that she would share my passion for running.

When we first started running together, my son, who is a couple years younger, was anxious to run too. I was cautious about having him start too soon, but in time he would join us. In a lifetime of unforgettable running memories, those runs with my kids rise above all the others.

Both of my children would follow in my running footsteps, but for my son, it was more of an activity than a sport. So, when he gave up spring track to try out for the high school play, I was happy to see him discover something he could feel more passionate about.

As a father, there have been many lessons I've tried to teach. I had a list of knowledge and experiences I wanted to transfer, but I'm afraid I've only been marginally successful. Life seems to teach better than I do.

There is something valuable, though, that I think my kids have gained from me: life is sweeter when you discover your passion and then live it faithfully.

Recently, I watched my son on the stage. He was charismatic and energetic. He was playful and engaging. He was brave and inspiring. In the words of a runner, he ran the perfect race.

Reflection is a valuable thing, isn't it? You see things differently when those things are behind you. And, experience gives you the blessing of foresight. I wish I could transfer that to my kids, but they'll have to learn about life the same way everyone else does – by living it.

On the other hand, foresight might be overrated. After all, I didn't even know what path these words would follow until I let my heart carry my fingers across the keyboard. And, if my kids can lead their lives in a similar way, I have a feeling they'll be just fine.

Chapter 2

Self-Confidence

Believing in One's Self

In the final miles of the first Bachman Valley Half Marathon, I caught up to Scott Douglas and we ran together to share the 1983 win. After coming back to win the race outright in '84 and '87, I came to the 1988 race with a feeling of confidence.

The course had hills in places where you didn't want them, but I knew those hills well. I had trained on the course hundreds of times with some of the same runners gathered at the starting line. Our sweat was sprinkled between the gravel of the roads. Looking back, the entire fall morning gave me a comfortable feeling of familiarity. Then the race started.

The early pack quickly dwindled to two of us, and I didn't know the man on my shoulder. When you are competitors in a race, you don't share much about yourself, so as he lingered a half stride off my pace, I felt like he was trying to hide himself.

Wanting to get back into familiar territory, I surged just after the fourth mile. I felt smooth as I ran under the trees of an old dirt road. The cool air on my face told me I was running well, and I passed the five-mile mark realizing I had covered that mile in less than five minutes. It was one of the finest miles I had ever run in a race of that distance, but there was a problem. He was still there.

It was at that point in the race when my confidence crumbled. Suddenly, I was running defensively and doubting my ability to keep up. I had to convince myself at each mile marker that I could stay with him until the next one. In the eleventh mile, I lost the mental battle, and he put a gap between us that held until the end of the race. In a time faster than any of my winning times, I would finish second.

In a brief conversation afterwards, I learned that my competitor was Steven Clark. Clark had just finished a successful college running career but had never raced longer than 10,000 meters. He had spent the entire race questioning his ability to cover the half-marathon distance. It was only recently that I understood the irony in that.

It's funny how life teaches lessons in its own time. I guess that has less to do with what we're capable of understanding and more to do with what we're willing to accept. Either way, I find myself wondering how well I could have run that day if I had simply believed in myself for the entire 13.1 miles.

18

Each year, runners return to the hills of the Bachman Valley Half Marathon. On the course, lessons are taught but sometimes not understood until many years later.

So, I'll keep reflecting on the races of my past. I'll keep remembering the victories and the disappointments. And, sometimes, new light will be shed on something that used to be unclear, and new hope will grow from the sweat that still stains the old gravel.

◆◆◆

Sam's wife had sent him for a few things at the grocery store, and he drove there trying to remember the brands she wanted. After he parked the car, he gulped down his last few ounces of Gatorade, wishing he had brought a second bottle along.

He noticed that the woman coming out of the store was watching curiously as he struggled to step up onto the curb. He smiled at her as she passed, owning the stiff ache from the morning run like a sign of honor.

Earlier, when the alarm had gone off at six, he resisted only briefly until he gained enough consciousness to realize he didn't have to go to work. He was out the door after downing a banana and some juice, leaving everyone else in the house still sleeping.

He had come to enjoy his Saturday morning runs more than any of the others. He felt a sense of satisfaction knowing he was accomplishing something when everyone else had yet to start their day.

He was going long this morning - twelve miles - and it would be the final long run before a half-marathon two weeks away. It was still hard to believe he was going to do it, when just a year before he couldn't run to the end of his street without walking.

Early in the run, the miles passed easily, and he spent much of the time watching the sun climb through various stages of dawn. It was only in the last few miles that he began to feel challenged. On the long runs, there was always a point when he wondered whether or not he could make it back home. He always did.

As he rounded the last turn and ran towards his house, a neighbor ventured out for the newspaper, first cup of coffee in hand. The neighbor said something like, "wish I had the time for such things," the irony apparently escaping him.

When he stopped running, the stiffness struck immediately, and he walked slowly up and down his driveway until he felt the steadiness return.

His wife had just made it to the breakfast table as he walked inside. She shook her head, still not understanding why he put himself through it all.

He didn't usually know how to explain it, but the words came more easily this particular morning. "I've spent most of my life," he told her, "trying to avoid a challenge. I've always steered clear of anything outside my comfort zone, but I'm not going to do that anymore. Running has taught me that I'm capable of more than I thought I was."

She asked him if he was capable of going to the store for a few things. Then, she kissed him, smiled, and said something he hadn't heard very often – "I'm proud of you."

He searched the aisles for the things she wanted, and even remembered all the brands. Then, he left the store grimacing as he stepped off the curb, carrying everything he needed, and then some.

♦♦♦

I remember a May race many years ago. It was a day when a lot of good things were coming together for me. I was beginning to understand how the specifics of my training translated into race results and I was applying what I knew in workouts. And, on this particular day with clear air and cool temperatures, I had chosen a race with just the right competition.

I was pulled through the first mile on the shoulder of a faster runner, and as we entered a downhill stretch we were flying. I felt smooth; the long, hard intervals on the track were paying off.

When things go perfectly in a race, there is little conscious thought. Thinking invites doubt and forces you to take an inventory of pain. It's to be avoided. In its place is concentration, a firm focus on the task at hand. For me, in this race, my single focus was holding on, and it resulted in the fastest 5,000 meters I had ever run.

I should have been ecstatic. Celebration should have been in order, but there was a problem. I was running a 10,000 meter race.

In a lifetime, there are moments that change life's course, whether subtly or with significance. For me, this was one of those moments. I could have decided that a 5K PR was enough and that jogging in the rest of the way was fine. I didn't do that.

The course turned onto a loop in a quiet park. There was no one there to watch us; it was only him and me, racing along the rolling road. I clung to his shoulder, refusing to let go and knowing, if I did, I would be left to watch him pull away.

I'm not sure I could describe the emotion I was feeling. It was almost like anger, but perhaps better described as intense determination.

We ran out of the park and began heading back towards the finish on the road we had come out on. Many runners had yet to enter the park, and they cheered as passed them, but their voices sounded far away, muffled by the concentration.

The last couple of miles were all out. I was just holding on, so as he surged near the finish, he pulled away to win by a few strides, but I finished just behind him with a huge personal best.

We all have a comfort zone, a safe room we usually avoid leaving, afraid of what might happen if we do. With preparation, we can expand its walls, but even then, our greatest potential never resides there.

That race taught me that my comfort zone is as much a confinement as it is a safe haven. Leaving it that day made me realize that I'm capable of more than I believed. And that simple understanding has stayed with me, giving me confidence whenever I've needed it, at least a thousand times since.

♦♦♦

It had been the topic of conversation all week – there was a snowstorm coming for the weekend. Knowing I'd never get my long run in once the storm kicked in, I decided to get it done on Friday within hours of when the storm was supposed to start.

I picked a quiet route where I knew there wouldn't be much traffic and started out slowly. Now that I'm older, it takes a mile or so for my body to remember I'm a runner. I used to fight that, didn't think a serious runner should plod along, but now I find it easier to treat my body like a partner rather than a subordinate. Before long, I was moving along in the normal rhythm.

The scene around me was nothing like you would have found in the grocery store that day. The world seemed at peace with whatever was coming. There were no leaves on the trees to hide the snow that lingered from the last storm, and I could see the full beauty of the landscape around me. I'm thankful I've never retreated to a treadmill when winter comes. Solitude is better when experienced in the midst of something bigger than you.

I pressed a little harder in the second half, remembering the benefit I was hoping to get from the run, but still feeling comfortable in the effort. As I moved along a

24

winding dirt road, the first flakes began to fall, and I knew I was one of the first to see the start of it. Within a few moments, the snow became steady, and I ran the last couple of miles in winter wonder.

When I got back home, I carried the peace with me. I don't know exactly how to describe it; I was simply ready to let myself get snowed in.

As I was waking up the next day, the news stations spoke of the epic storm. The snow was already piled up outside, still falling fast and blowing. Everyone else, like me, could do nothing but watch.

Usually, what's happening around us is beyond our control. Why then do we overreact, acting like we couldn't survive a day without milk and forgetting that melted snow makes water?

The truth is the only real control we have is self control. By believing in our own resilience and resourcefulness, the storms around us become less important.

The next great snowstorm came just days after the first one. It was an unprecedented event, and I couldn't resist the urge to run in it. I found a plowed path to follow and suddenly turned my focus away from what was raging around me and toward my ability to get through it.

There will always be storms. Challenges are abundant. Life is better when we accept that, stop wishing them away and start believing in ourselves. After all, something on the horizon is coming either way.

Chapter 3

Fortitude

Strength of Mind that Enables One to Endure Adversity

These words didn't come easily, but reluctantly, as if they didn't want to be heard. The thoughts and feelings formed a bottleneck, refusing to flow.

To start with, it was a week I had been dreading at work. I had to deliver difficult news and watch the emotional aftermath. Leadership has its drawbacks and leaves you standing alone sometimes.

As the week went on, I learned that several friends were dealing with loss. In one case, death had come just in time, almost mercifully. In another case it came far too swiftly, taking us by surprise. Afterwards, regardless of the details, loved ones grieved and wrestled with the unthinkable challenge of moving forward.

Others close to me were simply struggling with life itself, something we all do from time to time, but the abundance of sadness was unusual, as if sorrow was suddenly contagious.

Mixed in was the constant din of bad news and propaganda, media-driven noise that has led me to be far more cynical than I ever wanted to be. And it was all just too much. So, I turned to the stone foundation that has always kept me standing before.

There was no physical purpose for the run; I wasn't looking for a workout. So, as the stiffness lingered longer than usual, I simply ignored it. I didn't have the energy to run faster anyway.

I followed my normal route, not even thinking about where I was going. In fact, thought was absent; I was unconsciously going through the run, until movement on the trail ahead caught my attention. It was a young buck, his antlers just forming behind the ears that hadn't heard me approaching. He was slowly moving toward a wide stream, and I stopped so he wouldn't notice me.

He took a drink as a breeze freed some yellow leaves that danced to the ground around him. Then I was suddenly aware of the whole striking scene: the colors, the tranquility, and him standing in the middle, a body of growing strength. I didn't want to disturb it, didn't want the picture to change, so I turned around and headed back the other way.

Sometimes I get stuck in a figurative place and can't find my way out until running leads me in a better direction.

Whenever life turns ugly, running presents something beautiful. Whenever I feel weak, it gives me strength. I really don't know what I've done to deserve such a gift, but I'll accept it with gratitude.

When my run was over, nothing had changed, with the exception of my frame of mind, but that was enough to remove the bottleneck of thoughts and feelings and allow these words to form. Sometimes, trying to control life is a futile task, but I'm determined not to let it control me. And when it begins to take hold, I know exactly what to do.

◆◆◆

The clock beside the finish line was relentless, ticking along as Lori desperately tried to reach it in less than thirty minutes. It was a goal she had shared with me and the group that was waiting for her as she struggled in the final mile of the 5K race.

Her friend Stephanie got her to start running back in 2007. That's not unusual. Many people try running for the first time after being encouraged by a friend. After all, it takes courage to start as an adult, but this encouragement came in an unusual way.

Lori met Stephanie at her work, and within months they were best friends. At the time, both of them were struggling with the normal stresses of work and life, and a close friend added a foundation of comfort.

Stephanie was younger than Lori by about ten years, but that didn't seem to matter. She was smart and quick-witted, one of the funniest people Lori had ever known. Since both of their husbands were away during the evenings, they would go to Lori's house after work. Stephanie became part of Lori's family.

Over time, Lori learned about Stephanie's illness, juvenile diabetes. Stephanie had been on an insulin pump for years but didn't really take the disease seriously enough. When she developed an infection, she simply removed the pump and began using injections.

The details aren't really important. One day, Stephanie became shaky and disoriented. The next day, she was in a coma. Then she was dead. It was July 2007. Stephanie was 30 years old. She never ran.

For a while, Lori's world was empty. The part that Stephanie had filled was vacant until Lori learned about a diabetes 5K taking place that October.

Running was hard, but Lori found purpose in preparing for the race in Stephanie's honor. Early on, she had to get beyond her self-consciousness, but that didn't take long. Running soon became a new way to cope with life's hard issues.

Three years later, we waited for Lori at another finish line, the clock still moving toward thirty minutes. When we finally saw her in the distance, we weren't sure she would make it. She was pressing hard, but the seconds were ticking away. We screamed encouragement as she got closer.

Life takes its twists and turns. Sometimes we dream about what lies ahead and our dream comes true. Other times, we're unprepared. Whatever the case may be, life isn't so much about what lies around the next bend but about how we respond to what we find there. Lori met her goal with thirteen seconds to spare.

Time is relentless, like a clock at the finish line. If we knew what lies ahead, most of us would be more proactive. We'd take control of life. We'd do first things first and get beyond excuses.

Therein lies another secret that a running life unveils. Each day is an opportunity to find peace and clarity, and Lori finds that as she runs along, always remembering the friend who got her started.

◆◆◆

I was hurting, but no more than the other runners in the lead pack.

We had been climbing for nearly half a mile, about 200 meters from reaching the turnaround of a four mile race. The course was merciless, mostly downhill for the first mile and uphill for the second, and then reversed on the way back. The pack was bunched around me, all holding on and needing the relief that would come at the turnaround.

It was my final race of 1984, and I was finishing a breakout year, running several races that were perhaps the best I've ever run. My running log still has a note on the inside cover showing the goals I started the year with: 32:15 for 10K and 54:00 for ten miles. I had met one and came within seconds of the other.

When I look at that running log today, I wonder how I managed the mileage and the workouts. I long to feel the fluid motion I remember, as one run reinforced the next.

I was hurting on that hill, but I knew I had less pure speed than some of the other runners in the lead pack. On the downhill, they might use it to pull away, so I did the very opposite of what my body wanted me to do.

I sprinted, using the rest of the climb to put distance between us, and by the time I turned around they were scattered behind me, still struggling to reach the crest. They all looked at me with desperate stares, and I knew the race was already mine.

The adrenalin high on the decent was magnificent. The pain was gone. All I felt was freedom, as my legs moved on instinct. Near the base of the hill, I heard the footsteps of another runner, and he caught me briefly, but he had labored too hard to catch up. He was gone as soon as we began to climb, and I raced alone for the rest of the glorious way.

I know many would say that I'm lucky to have had the opportunity to win races, and I have to agree. In another respect, though, winning that race wasn't a gift; it was a return on investment.

Great opportunity doesn't present itself often. Sometimes, when it does, it will pass by untouched or even unrecognized. It is only with preparation that we can grasp a fleeting chance, and turn it into something great.

Running is a proving ground, a place where limits are tested, and capabilities are discovered. Through running, principles are learned that can be applied on race day, but more importantly, in life.

That's true for each and every runner, regardless of ability, because speed is a relative thing, but moral fiber isn't.

Some say that life has defining moments, but I think that's a misnomer. We are defined by the decisions we make, the work ethic we employ, and the discipline we display in the years before the moment happens.

We huddled together, gesturing to the camera that we were number one. The cold, damp air didn't seem to bother us by this time. Elation has a way of warming you.

We had just won the tri-state track and field championships by a margin that caused the reporter to use the headline "Blow Out City." To say we were proud would be an understatement.

I have to wonder if I would recognize many of the faces if I saw them now. The thirty years that have passed since the picture was taken have changed us, I'm sure. I wonder too if the rest of them remember that night, one I'll never forget.

When we arrived on the bus, the cold, steady rain had put my teammates in a lazy mood. Most of them were wishing the meet would be canceled when I stood up and voiced my anger. "Let the rest of the teams worry about the weather," I said. "Then, it will be to our advantage." As a senior, I didn't have many races left, and I had a lot yet to accomplish.

By the time I stood at the starting line for the mile that night, the rain had slowed to a drizzle. I was seeded third, behind two legendary runners. One, Kelly Long, had won the 4A cross country title the previous fall. The other, Jeff Scuffins, had dominated the track that season, and he would later win the Marine Corps Marathon in a course record of 2:14:01 that still stands.

The race went by in a muffled blur; I was aware only that I was on Scuffins' shoulder, running just off his pace. Each lap, the starter held up fingers to show how far we had yet to run. I paid little attention, trying only to hold on.

I don't remember much about the final lap, except that Scuffins began to pull away. I never once saw Long, who would finish third. I crossed the line between the two of them, propelling myself to a new status.

I've often wondered why I ran so well that night. Maybe I felt like I had to set the tone for my teammates. Maybe it was the urgency applied by my dwindling time in high school. Perhaps it was some combination of the two. All I know for sure is that I had never before been so focused. I didn't think at all. I just raced.

Too often, we all think too much. Between the day we are first told that we can accomplish anything we put our minds to and the day we realize that isn't so, we become subject to the most severe of all limitations - self doubt.

If that's true for you, let me ask you to use your imagination for a moment. Imagine that you and I are teammates. Together, we're waiting on a bus, while a cold, hard rain beats loudly on the roof.

Imagine the bus is your confinement. Imagine the rain is your obstacle. Listen as I tell you to stop thinking about the weather and to let that be the concern of others.

Now, from wherever you might be, step off the bus, find your starting line, and just race.

Chapter 4

Diligence

Constant and Earnest Effort

I watched her first high school race in the fall of 2003. She stood on that starting line without any expectations. I also watched her last high school race; she crossed the finish line of a journey that transformed her life.

Between her first race and her last, she found peace on the trails where she ran. She tested herself and overcame fears. She learned what it feels like to go beyond her wildest dreams, and she learned to deal with the disappointment of falling short. Each race offered its own challenge, each run a new opportunity. From the firing of that first starter's pistol to the very last home stretch, she grew with each passing stride.

Why is it that I watched her so closely? Well, I guess it's because I love her so much. It's because the sun rises and falls around her. It's because I was the first person to hold her the day I became her Dad.

My daughter excelled in school. She took courses that challenged her, and she responded to those challenges. She held leadership positions and earned the respect of her teachers and her peers. After high school, she went on to a prestigious college.

There will be times when what she learned in the classroom will not have prepared her for what lies ahead. There will be days when the workload is heavy and the deadlines are looming. There will be days when nothing is going right and success seems impossible. But she's ready for that, too.

She knows what it feels like to be in over her head and find the courage to get through. She knows that even when the hill seems to go on forever, there's a downhill on the other side. She knows that no matter how hard things may seem, the finish line lies ahead.

She has discipline and she knows that things of value aren't earned without sacrifice. Her greatest strength lies deep inside her, and she knows where to find it. So, when knowledge and reason and critical thinking just aren't enough, she has more than what she needs to muscle through.

Some time ago, we took a run together. We were on an isolated trail, and the only things near us were things you can find in any forest or near any lake. The miles passed easily as we talked about whatever it was that came to mind. It was peaceful, and any trouble we were facing just got further and further behind us.

And so, if all else fails, she knows she has that, too – the freedom to put it all behind her, clear her lungs and her mind, and come back with a fresh perspective. What could be more valuable than that?

I miss her. There is an emptiness not easily filled. I'll get over it in time, I know. And as I watch her run off toward what lies ahead, I know she's ready for whatever she finds. After all, my daughter is a runner.

◆◆◆

I started running in 1976, at a time when the American running boom was surging. Back then, Americans were competing with the best in the world, and I remember watching Frank Shorter enter the Olympic stadium in Montreal to win the silver medal. That was mildly disappointing after he had won the gold four years earlier in Munich.

Shorter was followed by a string of great American distance runners. Bill Rodgers, who had won the Boston Marathon for the first time in 1975, joined Shorter on the 1976 Olympic team and went on to win Boston three more times in 1978, '79 and '80. Then there was Alberto

Salazar, who would dominate the marathon distance, winning New York for three consecutive years from 1980 through 1982.

Among all the great distance runners of that time, I remember admiring Craig Virgin the most. In 1980, Virgin was the first, and still only, American to win the world cross-country title. He would do it again in 1981, the same year he finished second at Boston.

There was something else about Virgin, and I remembered it recently when I found an old video of him on the Internet. In the film, he was pulling away to win the 1981 Peachtree 10K in an American record time. As I watched it, it reminded me of – me.

Virgin and I looked alike. My own father once saw a picture of him in Runner Times Magazine and thought he was looking at a picture of his own son. There was something inspiring about that. I guess I figured if I looked like him, maybe I could run like him, too.

I spent many years trying. In the years that Virgin was winning races like Peachtree, I was beginning a string of local road racing wins. With each victory, my goals would elevate, and before long I was thinking I had a shot to run an Olympic Trials qualifying time.

It was a stretch, to say the least, but I was getting better every year and that goal kept me pressing forward.

It was a stress fracture that ended the string of successes. After that, life's changes pulled me away from running, and my focus was gone.

It was too difficult to dwell on giving up. From late childhood through my twenties, I wanted to be the next Craig Virgin, or at least the next closest thing.

What took me years to realize is this: that's not really what I wanted. I mean, I've never even met him. And while I'm sure he's a great guy, all I really know is that he ran fast. Still, all those years of wanting to be like him helped me do something pretty valuable. It helped me become me.

We all need role models. They inspire us. They give us direction, but it's important to follow them only until we discover our own way. Once we do that, we can lead instead of follow, and if we're lucky, become a role model ourselves.

◆◆◆

Cold rain is the worst weather to run in, and it was thirty-eight degrees and raining right outside my window. I watched it, wishing I didn't have a run planned.

In Maryland, the spring and fall offer the best running weather. The moderate temperatures feel perfect when contrasted with the extremes of the preceding seasons. On those days, I can't wait to get outside.

Of course, the transitional seasons have bad days as well. Temperatures go up and down, and dreariness moves in and out. Sometimes, it almost feels like summertime, when the weight of the damp heat makes me feel sluggish no matter how fit I am.

The truth is, if you tracked the weather throughout the year, there are really only a handful of perfect running days. So, I'm used to running in less-than-ideal conditions. I learned a long time ago that if I let the weather become an excuse, then I could find at least a hundred other excuses not to run. Excuses don't serve you well if there's something you hope to gain through persistence.

So, I stepped out into the rain. It wasn't any more pleasant than I imagined it would be. A hard breeze struck me with the first stride, and the rain stung my face. There wouldn't be any easing in to this run. I needed to move fast to warm up.

And I did warm up after ten minutes or so. By then, the

rain was more of a nuisance than a hindrance, and I was moving along in relative comfort.

That's the way it is when you're facing something difficult. The hardest part is almost always the very first step. Once you're moving in the right direction, momentum becomes a friend.

People passing in their cars didn't understand. They looked at me with curiosity, wondering why anyone would willingly be outside. They had no idea I was feeling comfortable, the hardest part of the run well behind me.

I eased through the final mile and turned onto my street, stopping at my driveway. I felt a sense of gratification and even stood for a few moments feeling the rain fall before going back inside.

If you are like me, you probably reflect on the past every once in a while. Time passes quickly, and it is easy to think that we've lost the promise of days past. Sometimes, that kind of reflection can lead to regret. Don't let it.

Instead, focus on the years ahead and the unwritten chapters of your life. What is it that you want to do? And perhaps more importantly, who is it that you want to become? Now is a time to imagine and to dream, not to lament.

When you do dream, paint a picture of yourself in the fulfillment of your vision.   Let that picture preside over the days ahead because, rest assured, you'll need the motivation when the cold rain comes. And it will come, forming an obstacle between you and your dream. Move ahead in spite of it. Its sting is temporary, but the gratification that comes from running through it endures.

Chapter 5

Discipline

The Trait of Being Under Control

It was four o'clock on a Friday afternoon, and I decided to leave the pressure of the workweek a little earlier than normal. I grabbed my running bag and walked towards the locker room in my office building.

I was celebrating a promotion, a milestone I didn't think I'd reach in my career, and a short run at the end of the workweek seemed like an appropriate self-indulgence.

As I began my run, I had no company on the pathway except for the flock of geese that scattered as I approached. They flew to the middle of a large pond, and as they hit the icy water, I was glad I wasn't one of them.

I didn't have any particular route planned. Instead, I wandered from place to place. I ran past the track where I've done some of my hardest workouts and by the trail where I've found peace away from many hectic mornings.

I was running easily, trying to reflect on what I had just accomplished, and in the middle of the run something unexpected occurred to me. My run wasn't as much a celebration as it was a tribute to the thing that has contributed more to my personal success than anything else I can name.

Based on my education and background, I've climbed much higher up the corporate ladder than I ever should have, and I have the discipline of running to thank for that.

I never once believed that someone or something else was responsible for my success. Running taught me long ago that there is danger in that kind of thinking. The moment you leave your future in the hands of things outside of your control, is the moment you place it in the hands of circumstance. And circumstance doesn't much care about your success.

Running has also taught me that adversity is better faced head-on than avoided. The hill in front of you won't go away, but it's easy enough to put it behind you if you just press harder for a while. Call it discipline or call it determination; without it you won't get very far.

That lesson isn't taught enough, and too many people never realize that sacrifice is a requirement of life. You either sacrifice today to reach tomorrow's goals, or you give up your dreams in favor of the fleeting comfort that's distracting you. The pleasant reality, for those

46

who choose the former, is that comfort is abundant when long-term goals are achieved.

When my run was finished, I went back inside and took a quick shower. I walked back to my office to grab my briefcase before heading home. I said goodbye, wondering if anyone even noticed that I had been gone during my run.

The following Monday, when I arrived back at work, I looked outside my office window and saw the geese gathered around the pond. I watched them for a few moments before getting my day started.

As I went about my morning, I faced pressing challenges, gave guidance to the people around me and tried to create a vision for what lies ahead.

Then, when lunchtime rolled around, I grabbed my running bag and spent some time strengthening the disciplines through which I've earned the privilege to do all those things.

♦♦♦

Each fall, as the long evenings of summer suddenly fade, I'm reminded that time is passing more quickly than I realized.

Of course, time is a constant; it ticks away at the same pace it always has. A minute is still sixty seconds, just like it was when the first flower bloomed in the spring. Distance is another constant; a mile is 1,760 yards away, no matter which direction you travel. It always has been and always will be.

Running brings together these two great constants, time and distance. It's pure that way. Running, simply put, is about the measurement of time and distance.

There's something reassuring to me about that. I'm not sure what it is, but in a world that seems too complex, I'm glad that I can define my passion in simple terms.

And yet, as simple as running may be, there is something complex about the runner. Each individual comes to running with different dreams, unique motivations and personal challenges. And each one seeks to explore their own potential by measuring themselves against distance and time.

Discovering potential as a runner isn't easy; potential has a way of hiding itself. Sometimes, it can take years of hard work just to begin to recognize it. Then, even after decades of running, the runner never really knows if his potential has been reached, which may be why so many of us have a deep-rooted need to keep running.

The purity of running and the complexity of the runner are things that transcend generations. Recently, I had a chance to meet a small group of young, dedicated runners. The discussion turned, as it does many times, to the subject of racing times.

In an instant, each one of us could appreciate the accomplishments of the others because a mile and a minute are the same today as they were years ago. And because every runner understands what it takes to develop potential.

We all need to measure ourselves in one way or another. Some resist, afraid of what the outcome might be, but I think they're selling themselves short. Almost without exception, each individual's potential goes beyond their own expectations, and potential can only be reached by those willing to measure their progress towards it.

Maybe runners have it easy. Time and distance are easy to measure. Personal growth, on the other hand, is harder to assess, but I've learned through running that growth in one way naturally leads to growth in another. After all, as you watch a tree reach ever closer toward the sky, don't you understand that the roots are growing stronger and deeper as well?

The transition between the seasons always reminds

me that time keeps moving forward. Whenever that happens, I remember how important it is for me to define a destination and to measure my progress towards it.

◆◆◆

Two runners live inside me. The first one runs without effort, smooth and fast. He is focused, his energy channeled with precision, wanting only to improve.

He is a fierce competitor, daring and tenacious. He lives for brief, glorious moments, like the instant when a competitor's footfalls first begin to fade behind him. His expectations are unquenchable. Seldom is he satisfied, even when he wins.

I remember how he led me to running back in high school, that first race when he helped me keep pace with the older runners. And later, he pushed me far beyond my expectations, each race another chance to prove something more.

It would be easy now for him to dismiss me; I can't offer what he needs. And yet he stays nonetheless, encouraging me to try.

The second runner can go for miles without thinking once about speed. He thrives on the motion, the simple rhythm that makes him feel at home. He seeks peace, not recognition.

Through his eyes, I've watched beautiful scenes, pastures, mountains and wildlife that the first runner would scurry past. There are times when he'll stop, just to spend a few extra moments fixed within the gaze of a deer.

He was born from the first. He never would have existed without him, and yet he's matured far beyond his predecessor. He is wise, understanding the connections between running and life. And so, each run is a simple pleasure, just as each day is another gift to a life.

Independently, I am forever bonded with both runners, but when they come together there is conflict. I feel torn, wrestling with our relationship like a parent wrestles with sibling rivalry. I try to compromise, but with little influence. I suffer the yearnings of the first runner and minimize the wisdom of the second.

I have relied on the second runner for a long time now as injury and age have cursed me with limitation. And, in an irony I can't exactly explain, it is he who has gifted me with the patience I needed to persist long enough to give the first runner new life.

During the years when the injuries threatened to take

running from me, it was he who gave me reasons to keep going. It was he who showed me that I can endure more miles when I don't press on every run. Because of him, I have a new base of fitness. I feel ready to consider racing again.

I need them both. I must find a way to bring them together, to resolve their differences and make them one. It won't be easy, but running has taught me that nothing worthwhile ever is.

Perhaps I can be disciplined enough to take the best from each of them. I can find the peace that my busy life so desperately demands and still have brilliant moments, when my stride opens up and I run free. And if I am successful, it can be better than it's ever been before.

◆◆◆

Heat and bronchitis are not friends of a distance runner, but I had to deal with both in May of 1979.

I was finishing a fantastic senior year of high school. After more than three years of striving just to place, I was finally winning races. I was determined not to let the conditions impact the end of my season.

Running the mile at the district meet, I tucked into the pack early on and then ran just off the lead. The race went by quickly, but as we began the final lap I was feeling the effort more than I'd hoped. The leader began to pull away, and I had to push hard to finish third.

Unhappy, I walked away from the track, not knowing my high school running career was over. The illness got worst in the days that followed, and the doctor encouraged me not to compete at the state meet. I wish I hadn't listened, but then again, who doesn't have some regrets about those days?

As graduation approached, I found myself struggling. I had everything I wanted; I was surrounded by the friends I loved and I had finally found the running success I'd been craving. What lay ahead of me was uncertain and scary. I didn't want to move on.

Now, more than thirty years later, I'm watching my children pass through their own difficult transitions. How is it, in a world that's constantly changing, that human struggle stays the same?

Of course, a father can only provide so much direction. They want to find their own way just like the rest of us. Even if I still remember the apprehension and the fear, theirs is unique and personal. As much as I'd like to, I can't take it away from them.

When I was their age, dealing with change was anything but easy. Each new situation presented different challenges. A new relationship caused me to present myself in a way I thought was expected. I was confused about how all that should work.

Over time, running helped me gain clarity because I began to form myself around its principles. I chose things like personal responsibility, discipline, and loyalty as core values. And, somewhere in my journey an important secret became clear to me; what you leave behind and what you move towards are unimportant when compared to what is carried within you.

That is a valuable thing to understand. Life is a constant process of transition, even if it's only apparent in the vivid beginnings and endings we experience. And yet, if we've built ourselves around stable values, we can be strong in the midst of change, because we ourselves stay the same.

I'm lucky. Each time I feel the familiar motion and effort of a run, my stability is reinforced.

I do worry about my kids, but I probably don't have to. I see them forming and living by their own principles. So, as they continually face a changing world, they can stand reassured and true.

Chapter 6

Determination

Firmness of Purpose

Bob Ward didn't want his parents to see his final college race in 2002. He didn't think they would want to watch it, so he asked them not to come. Looking back now, he regrets that more than anything.

A few months earlier, during his senior indoor track season for Widener University, he had done some of the best racing of his life. Having already qualified to compete in the 800 meter race at the outdoor conference meet, he was hoping to help his team win its fourth straight conference championship.

He spent the week between seasons home on spring break. While there, he used the time to get some distance in as he prepared to start his final track season, but his last run before heading back to Widener would change the course of things.

A truck failed to stop at a red light. Bob doesn't know much more than that, except that he was in its path. The police report said it was going fifty miles an hour when it hit him. I spoke to one of Bob's friends, a paramedic, who was on the scene and didn't recognize him at first. He wondered if Bob would survive as he watched the Medevac helicopter carry him away.

His injuries were extensive, but he was in the best shape of his life, and that helped him recover at a rate that surprised everyone. Still, a broken femur bone made the doctors caution Bob against considering anything more than walking as a goal.

He was sent home with a wheelchair and a set of crutches, and two days later, with the help of his father, he went outside to hobble along the sidewalk on the crutches. That's the moment he decided he wanted to join his team and run at the conference meet.

Even after he returned to college, the most optimistic doctor told him it would take six months before he could run again. But each day, Bob was dedicated to his therapy, knowing he couldn't run until his doctors gave their approval. Finally, just before the championship meet, they did.

You can imagine the scene as Bob walked towards the starting line. Everyone in the stadium seemed to know his story, and they lined the track waiting to encourage him.

The 800 meters is just a two-lap race, and perhaps the most amazing fact is that Bob wasn't lapped. He doesn't even remember the pain, the adrenalin and the crowd shielding him as he ran the slowest but most heroic race of his life.

We tend to celebrate the victorious, people who give us stunning performances. It's fitting that we do this. After all, champions help us envision our own potential. On the other hand, gold medals tarnish, as do the reputations of far too many of the people who win them. Maybe that's why I've come to value the inspiring over the accomplished, humility more than triumph.

I can't tell you how many people Bob inspired that day, other than to say it was many. And while few even remember the names of the champions, everyone who was there remembers Bob's race. He only wishes his parents were among them. In some larger sense, though, I'm certain they were.

I didn't recognize the name of the sender, but the postmark showed that it was from Pittsburgh. Whatever was inside, it had traveled more than 200 miles to reach me.

The card contained a hand-written note from the mother of a runner I coach. She told me that she enjoyed my running column and expressed appreciation for my support of her daughter's running. It was a nice surprise.

I first met her daughter, Danielle Schwessinger, when she joined the Flying Feet Summer Running program. She had been running for a while, but not as regularly as she wanted. Through the summer, her mileage increased every week and she surpassed her own goal. It was a pleasure watching her fitness improve and her love of running grow.

When Danielle joined the fall program, I was impressed to learn that she wanted to run a ten-mile race. It was a lofty goal for someone with her limited running experience, but it didn't take long to realize that she was up to the challenge.

When I told Danielle about the note, I began to understand why her mother had such appreciation for my running programs. Danielle's father had been diagnosed with lung cancer when she was just sixteen years old, and from her mom's perspective, running was a means to a long, healthy life.

Her father had been a strong provider – a driven man. He worked long hours to achieve success. It was only in the months of his illness that Danielle had gotten to know him well. She came to admire his strength and his sense of humor, and then he was gone.

To avoid the pain, Danielle immersed herself in the hard work of a student. It was only after college that life forced her to slow down and deal with the loss. That's when she started to run.

Running gave her peaceful time to reflect. She began feeling better physically and emotionally. And, most surprisingly, there were times when she felt her dad running beside her, as if he were finally there again, encouraging her along.

I have to wonder if he somehow planted the idea to run ten miles. Maybe he understood that his daughter needed a goal to pursue. Maybe he wanted her to discover her own full potential. Perhaps he wanted her to experience life in ways he never could.

It traveled 200 miles to reach me - a note that delivered a story I didn't understand at first.

We all have a story, don't we? For most of us, it speaks of challenge. Life is never easy, even for the most fortunate among us. I've come to realize that this is how it's supposed to be. It is only through struggle that we grow.

Danielle has discovered what many runners have learned before her – running strengthens a spirit. It builds courage. It prepares a person for the challenges of life.

As she crossed the finish line, the soul of a man with nicotine-black lungs breathed once again to whisper a message of love into the heart of his daughter. Now, she runs on with a sense of satisfaction, finally knowing how proud he's always been.

◆◆◆

Name a city, any city. Name Baltimore, Pittsburgh or Philadelphia, and I think of high-rise buildings, crowded city streets and a place this country boy doesn't want to be. Name a city, any city. That is, except Boston. Name Boston and I think of something else.

The historic Boston Marathon is run every April. To enter, you need to do more than pay an entry fee. You have to qualify by running a marathon faster than the challenging qualifying times. Though the standards have been softened over the years to allow more runners to enter, only the best earn the privilege of running on the streets of Boston.

The first Boston Marathon that I remember watching was in 1982. The world record holder, Alberto Salazar, dueled with Dick Beardsley, a relatively-unknown dairy farmer from Minnesota. I watched in awe as they ran sub-five-minute miles, the giant versus the underdog. Beardsley tried to run away, but he could see Salazar's shadow beside him. As the miles passed, it was clear that neither man was willing to relent. It was only in the final meters that the outcome was decided – the king would keep his crown. But Dick Beardsley taught me a lesson that day. <u>To truly find out what you can accomplish, you've got to push yourself into unknown territory.</u>

A couple years later, I entered the Marine Corps Marathon in hopes of searching the unknown myself. I had a big goal but faltered late in the race to finish in 2:44. Disappointed, I decided to wait a while before trying another marathon, and though I had qualified for Boston by running faster than the 2:50 standard, I decided to take a pass.

As fate would have it, seventeen years went by before I ran my next marathon. Inspired by my fortieth birthday, I figured it was time to try again. Running 3:06 and bettering the 3:20 standard for a master, I qualified for Boston a second time. But I decided the timing wasn't right. A few years later an arthritic knee made me wonder if I would ever complete another marathon. My chances to run Boston seemed to be past. And so, when the gun fires each year in April, you know what I'm thinking.

Regret is a painful thing. It reminds you that you made a mistake. You made a bad choice. You should have taken another path. Fortunately, I have very few – regrets, that is. But name the city of Boston, and that's what comes to mind. It's kind of funny that a race I never ran has taught me so much. Dick Beardsley saw to my first lesson, and I guess I have myself to thank for the rest.

In more recent years, I've worked hard to overcome the troubled knee. While it still places limitations, the disappointment of the past has become the fuel of determination.

And if I do qualify for Boston again, you know where I'll be the following April.

Chapter 7

Resilience

The Ability to Recover

It was a simple compliment. Dave Herlocker was saying goodbye to me after I had directed a local race, and he said matter-of-factly, "You're a good man, Dave." I don't know why, but I've never forgotten that. I guess compliments mean the most when they come from someone you respect.

The depth of my admiration for Dave was formed in a unique way, and I can place it back to a specific morning in 1995 that began with the thump of a Medevac helicopter passing over my house. As I sat at my breakfast table that morning, I didn't understand the significance of the moment. I simply sat and listened to it slowly fade away; but I haven't heard the sound since without thinking about Dave.

Earlier that morning, he was running with his buddies. It was a frequent routine. They would talk about their lives, throw verbal jabs and laugh as they ran. Then they would move on to start a normal day, but this particular day wouldn't be ordinary.

The accident must have happened in the moments just before I heard the helicopter. The driver had been drowsy for a while before falling asleep. His car swerved across the road, then onto the shoulder, where Dave and his friend Terry ran. Dave, who was running just ahead, was hit first and then violently pushed into Terry.

Those who were on the scene said that the paramedics worked frantically on Dave, while Terry seemed to be in better shape, even standing up on his own. Later, at the hospital, Dave continued to fight for his life when the most surprising news of all came – Terry didn't make it. I began preparing myself to lose two friends, but Dave surprised us all. He fought on like a runner.

The months that followed were harder than anyone should be asked to endure, but he would somehow live through it all. Still, as if the pain wasn't enough, the accident required another unfair sacrifice; Dave would never run again.

I can only imagine how much he must have missed it. And yet, you couldn't tell from being around him. He returned to be the heart and soul of the Westminster Road Runners Club. He directed or helped at nearly every local race and shared the excitement of any running accomplishment that was achieved by a local runner.

Dave's effort and passion moved through my running community like blood runs through our veins.

Many mornings, I saw Dave taking a long, brisk walk with his dogs. It didn't matter what the conditions were; Dave's runner's heart brought him out with an inspiring dedication. Even more remarkably, he would compete in many events, usually starting ahead of the runners to avoid making the finish line crew wait for him to finish. I watched many times as Dave pressed his limits, needing still to get the very best from himself.

Whenever I've seen Dave limping towards me, I've realized that I was watching one of the strongest men I've ever known, and one of the bravest, too. And each time I've wondered if I possess the same incredible endurance that allowed him to survive and succeed through such tragedy. The answer has always been the same – I don't think so.

I can't hear the thump of a Medevac helicopter without remembering that morning long ago. And now, there's another morning I'll remember with even more sadness.

I was reading email like I normally do before getting my day started, and I saw an email on the list with a title that simply read "Dave Herlocker." I was scared to open it, and it turned out my instinct held true. Dave had passed away quietly in his home.

It seems ironic that a man who fought so hard to live through tragedy would pass on in peaceful sleep. Life really is curious while you're living it.

The curiosities of this life are behind Dave now, just like the pain he's endured. And if I close my eyes, I can see him smiling as he stands on his old runner's legs. Can you imagine the exhilaration he must feel?

Now the pain is in those he left behind. For me, it is eased as I imagine what Dave is doing at this very moment. He's with Terry, bringing him up-to-date on everything new. They're laughing and teasing as they take the longest, fastest and best run they've ever shared.

Thanks for that compliment, Dave. I'll never forget it. And if it's not too much trouble, make a note on some future calendar so that we can take a long run together and so that I can return the favor.

Patti hated the hill, but she couldn't take a run without having to climb it. Her house stood at the crest.

This day, as she saw it looming in front of her, she wasn't sure she could make it up. She felt weak, her strength left back at the house where she had been fighting again with her teenage son. They had lived alone now for almost a year, and it hadn't been easy.

The hill was nearly a mile long, mostly gradual. There were a couple places where it leveled off, and there was a steep rise near the top. She approached it thinking how hard things had been and wanting to give up, even stopping at the foot of it.

She stood listening to her breath break the silence of the morning. Clouds drifted from her mouth with each exhale, and she watched them float off and disappear. She wished she could disappear like that.

The first step was just as sluggish as the last one, and she felt the hill pushing against her. She had no choice but to push back, and a small burst of energy came from somewhere just before she made it to the first plateau.

She relaxed for a few moments before the hill began to climb again, and then she felt a surge of emotion rise inside herself. She heard her own voice say, "Damn this hill."

Her speed was nearly twice what it had been, determination pushing her forward. Her arms pumped

67

with each stride, punching the air. She didn't back off at the next plateau, and she felt herself accelerate as she came to the last rise.

Suddenly, she felt good, soothed by the rhythm of the motion. She looked to the side and watched the trees speed by as she passed, then looked ahead to the final, steep climb.

She was almost sprinting when she made the crest and considered continuing on past the house, before she thought about her son again. She should get back inside.

She stood in her driveway looking back at the hill as her breathing settled down. She thought about the irony. How could she be void of energy at the bottom of the hill and filled with it at the top? She didn't know. All she could think was, "Maybe I don't hate that hill as much as I thought I did."

As she turned toward the house, she saw the face of her son in the window. She stopped, smiling as it dawned on her – he has his own hills to climb.

As she stepped into the house and towards her son, she remembered why she started running almost a year ago. She needed the brief escape and the peaceful air. Now, she knew she was getting that and more.

She hugged her son, and they spoke together like they hadn't spoken in a long time. They talked about hills.

◆◆◆

It started as a challenge between friends.

Art was one of our training partners, but he was also an excellent cyclist. The rest of us were hard-core runners, and we didn't give Art much respect for his cycling. In fact, we teased him constantly.

Art competed in a 105-mile bike race each year that covered the back roads between Kent Island and Ocean City, Maryland, and our challenge to him was simple. Three of us - Jim, Frank and I - would cover the same 105-mile course by running it as a relay team. Since we didn't have wheels, we would begin running at midnight, five hours before the start of the bike race. Whoever got to Ocean City first would win bragging rights. Art accepted.

When the night of the challenge finally came, I remember standing in the midnight darkness as Art kept us honest about our starting time. Frank took the first leg, and Jim and I climbed into the van that would transport the two of us who weren't running at any given time.

I ran second, and I stood on the side of the road waiting

for Frank to touch my hand. Then, I was running down an old, back road in what seemed like the middle of nowhere. My heart raced as I watched the van pull away, the taillights disappearing behind a faraway turn, and I was alone.

I don't ever remember feeling more excitement on a run. I was moving fast, pushed forward by exhilaration. It was pitch-black, and I couldn't help wondering what was watching from the fields surrounding me.

We took turns through the night, and we had over fifty miles behind us by the time we knew Art was getting started.

The road slowly became more visible as the sun rose, but the air warmed quickly. By early morning, we were running in muggy, summer heat, and at a time when water was kept in a jug, not in little bottles, it was the beginning of the end when our water was suddenly lost. (It's a long story. Frank would be glad to give you the details.)

I can't remember exactly how far we had gone when it was my turn to run and I couldn't go. I took a stride, and dehydration caused me to double over with cramps. After a short discussion, we decided we had to stop.

We waited for Art to ride by. He was struggling but got a

boost when he saw us. He earned those bragging rights, and I guess we deserved the ribbing that came with it.

We talked for a while about a rematch, but life took its turns, just like it always does, and there never was another challenge.

From time to time, I remember a day I wish I could live over again. Sometimes, it's because I'd like to bring back the pleasure of an experience. Other times, I'd just like another chance to do better. In this case, both apply.

Of course, going back in time is just wishful thinking. So, I'll have to settle for closing my eyes and remembering a long, dark, winding road where running tested my spirit, just like so many other times before and since.

My first running buddy was a miniature schnauzer named Pepper. Pepper was my childhood dog, my companion growing up. I don't remember very much about him anymore, with the exception of a few things and, more importantly, how I felt about him. We were bonded like many young boys and their dogs.

He was chosen as my running buddy by default. There was no one else who wanted to play running with me, so he joined in, though reluctantly at times.

The race course consisted of circles around our house. Given that Pepper was on a leash and didn't know how many laps were in the race, I had a distinct advantage. He would normally run a few yards ahead, and then I would heroically sprint past him just before the finish line. We would celebrate together, the winner and the runner-up.

I'm not sure how old Pepper was when he got sick. All I remember is sitting at the table crying with my mother and sister as my father carried him out of the house. He died before I got to high school and became a real runner.

Growing up is hard; I doubt anyone would dispute that. Relationships are risky from the beginning. Friends come and go with the passing of school years and the making of young decisions. It's no wonder we all struggle through that time as we search for affirmation through other kids who are mostly incapable of giving it. In times when I needed it most, Pepper was waiting.

The first gift running provided was the blessing of self-confidence. I faced challenges. I struggled, but I overcame them and found success. The days of needing someone else to assure me were past.

Later, when I was learning to live with the pressure of life's routines and deadlines, running gave me stability in a changing world. Every day there was a break in the madness when I went outside to play.

Running gave me freedom. It let me dream. It formed a bridge between my childhood and adulthood that helped me keep my identity as my peers were losing theirs.

When my kids were young, it seemed natural to get a dog for them. We chose a bischon because it seemed like the breed was a perfect match for our family. We named him Forrest after the then-famous runner Forrest Gump.

Not surprisingly, Forrest formed a strong bond with my son. Forrest is to him as Pepper was to me.

I'm always amazed at how quickly the years pass, and Forrest is fourteen now. He's showing signs that the end is coming. And so, life will repeat itself like it does sometimes, and I'll be the father carrying the dog away as family members watch with tears in their eyes.

Even if we don't realize it, the pieces of life are connected together. Our childhood, our relationships and our experiences live on in us, even after they've passed on. I've come to understand that, for some, those memories form anchors, holding them in place as life passes by.

Somehow, I've managed to keep all of life's challenges in perspective and keep moving forward, and I have a feeling I have running to thank for that.

Chapter 8

Patience

Ability to Endure Delay

This story isn't over, just so you know. The final chapters will only be written in time.

I'll begin the telling with a photograph, taken just moments before the start of the 2009 Baltimore Half-Marathon. Julie Peatt is with the rest of the runners I coach, easy to spot wearing a purple birthday hat. It was her 46th birthday, and the day was made even more special because she had missed this race the year before. After having trained since early summer 2008, a hip injury made it impossible for her to run.

The day before the 2009 race, Julie browsed through the exhibits at the runner's expo looking for a meaningful souvenir. She found two: a magnet with a quote from John Bingham that reads "The miracle isn't that I finished - The miracle is that I had the courage to start," and a bracelet with the inscription "Trust the journey." She's worn the bracelet nearly every day since.

After the picture was taken, Julie went to the starting line with her running partners. If you've never been to an event like this one, you'll have a hard time imagining the experience. Thousands of runners were waiting for a moment that had taken months, sometimes years, to prepare for. When the race finally began, the burden of apprehension was collectively lifted from the crowd.

Julie and her partners began easy, remembering not to get caught up in the excitement. There was a point early on when a motivating song played over the crowd, and Julie pulled away briefly before regaining control and slowing down to re-join her friends.

By the time she got to mile seven, a familiar pain in her hip was becoming increasingly uncomfortable. As she passed mile eight, it was impossible to ignore. Just before mile nine, severe pain stopped her in her tracks. Her hip labrum, the cartilage lining the hip socket, had torn.

The events that followed were blurry. There was a period of walking and jogging when Julie tried to convince herself she could still finish. Friends would pass and she urged them on, telling them that she would see them at the end. There was an old college friend at a water stop and a couple police officers who offered to help. Finally, a running friend made her face the reality – she needed to stop.

There is another picture from that day as she waited in the ambulance, waving to the camera and still wearing the purple birthday hat. That picture, as much as anything else, might tell you something about Julie.

It doesn't really matter that she didn't finish. She did have the courage to start, which is far more important. Too many times, we're unwilling to leave the safety of our comfort zone, and that confinement places a greater limitation on our lives than any other thing.

And once you do find the courage, understand that you may never reach your destination - but that's okay. A destination marks a moment in time, a brief conclusion, but the journey is life itself.

Cautiously now, Julie returns to running, living the final chapters of an unfinished story and trusting the journey as she goes.

◆◆◆

I had to stop. The urge was so strong that I didn't want to fight it anymore. So I did - stop running, that is.

I didn't realize it was going to be a bad run when I started. It began much like most of my other midweek, lunchtime runs. All I was looking for was a quiet escape from the morning rush, and I ran slowly, moving towards my favorite trail.

Before I had even finished the first mile, I could tell I wasn't going to be picking up the pace. My legs were heavy. My breathing was labored. I tried to distract myself by looking at the landscape, but it didn't help very much.

I made it to the point where I turn around, and I started heading back. I wondered why I was struggling, when just the day before my run had been a good one. Then, I felt relaxed and fast, which reminded me of my running before the accumulating years slowed me down.

I knew well enough, after more than thirty years of running, that sometimes I simply won't know exactly what it is that's slowing me. It could be emotions or restless sleep. It could be the remnants of greasy food from days before, still lingering in the muscles I was asking to propel me forward. Whatever the reason, there was nothing that I could do to change it.

And so, I was left with a single choice: to accept it. Less than a mile from finishing, I stopped.

I walked slowly along the pathway, listening to my breathing settle down. As it faded, I heard the playful noise of nature rising - simple joy that always exists for those who look closely enough.

When I was younger, I never would have allowed myself the pleasure of backing off. I would have thought I was weak for doing so. Now, I think I'm a little wiser. Energy is a limited resource, and investing it foolishly has never gotten me very far.

It's taken me longer than it should have, but I've finally learned that bad days are simply a part of the deal. You can't win unless you're willing to lose. And, though most people never sort through the irony, you can't take control of your life until you're willing to accept that some things are simply outside of your control.

No one ever achieved anything by applying their effort or worry towards something they can't influence. After all, you can't move an ocean, no matter how large your bucket might be. Success, then, is only achieved by continually channeling your energy towards the things you can influence, like making sure you start moving forward again after a brief reprieve.

I took a deep breath and started running again. My legs moved a bit more freely than before, and I was able to enjoy the final moments of a run I was glad to finish.

The fatigue lingered for a little while, but before long my tired run was forgotten. I moved on to more productive things and began looking forward to my next run.

◆◆◆

He was just finishing his workout as I ran onto the track, and it just so happened that we both stopped to stretch at the same place and at the same time. I asked him how he was doing, and I could feel the frustration in his response.

He was young, maybe 20, and I could tell he was a good runner. His talent was equaled by his passion, so my heart went out to him as he told me about the challenges he was facing.

He could hardly get through the workout he had just finished, and his times were slower than he was shooting for. It had been like that for a while, and he couldn't seem to break away from the sluggishness. He wanted it to be like it had been when he was running well and improving consistently.

When he was ready to walk away, I found myself wanting to offer something that would help, but all I could manage was, "Hang in there. Things will get better."

As I started my own workout, I began thinking about the missed opportunity. I had a chance to have an impact on this young runner, and I wondered if I had been helpful at all.

I spent the rest of my workout thinking about how I used to feel when my stride wasn't restricted by old joints. There were times when it seemed like I could have run as fast and as far as I wanted. I remember dreaming about faster times and then accomplishing the workouts that would lead toward my goals. Races were playgrounds.

I also remember when it hadn't been so easy. There were long stretches, sometimes a year or more, when I couldn't find rhythm in my running.

When my workout was over, I stopped in the same spot to stretch again, and I noticed he had left his sweatshirt behind. Just as I was about to leave, I saw him walking toward me.

There was an awkward moment as he wondered why I was waiting for him, but it dissolved in to good conversation as I shared my story. I think it helped him to know that what he was going through wasn't unusual.

Then I told him something that he wasn't expecting, something he might not understand until a few more years pass by. The human spirit has a deep-rooted need to be tested, and potential can never be fully realized until the spirit is strong. So, I told him, even as hard as things seemed, he was developing in ways he might not yet fully appreciate, and the worst thing he could ever do is give up.

Some people think that life would be better if things always went exactly the way we wanted them to, but I'm not convinced that's true. Fulfillment would be hard to find in a world where success was handed out like free samples at the grocery store.

So, as you crave what you want in life, try to understand that the journey towards success is just as important as whatever prize you're chasing. After all, in the end, it's not really what you get that matters; it's what you become.

Chapter 9

Accountability

Willingness to Accept Responsibility

The September morning was a stark contrast to the summer-like days leading up to it. The air was crisp, perfect for the 10K race I was about to run.

My training had been going well. I had put in three straight weeks of sixty or more miles, something I rarely did. My track work had been strong as well, perhaps better than it had ever been before.

We started on the streets of the small town hosting the race, and the first mile led us onto country roads close by. Early on, I was letting the race unfold without much thought with the leaders running about 30 yards ahead. That's when the runner beside me said matter-of-factly – "Let's catch those guys."

Together, we surged up to the leaders, and within minutes I was controlling the pace up front. From that point on, I remember feeling like I was floating along the course. By the two mile mark, there were just two runners struggling to hold on, and I smiled as the marshal called out the split. I knew already that the race was mine.

It's pretty special knowing something great is happening and having time to relish the experience. I turned around at the 5K mark and began the journey back. I could feel the eyes of my competitors, and as I ran on through the fourth mile, I heard cheers from the crowd of runners still moving out towards the turnaround.

As I passed back into city limits, a police motorcycle began to escort me toward the center of town. I followed it, feeling myself picking up the pace. There was a final rise, then a descent to the finish where I couldn't help but raise my arms as I crossed the line with a personal best.

Some might say that remembering a day like that is basking in old glory, but there are more important reasons to reminisce.

Before that race, I placed limits on what I could accomplish, and I had dreams that I doubted would ever come true. Afterwards, I found a reason to believe in myself, and dreams that seemed unreachable were suddenly in the realm of possibility. Why would I want to forget a day like that?

I already knew that hard work and diligence were parts of the success equation, but I learned that day that accountability was a missing piece; I couldn't wait for someone else to tell me when it was time to run with the leaders.

Every time I look back on my best races, I find a lesson worth remembering. It's like a seed was planted each time, and it's only in looking back that I can discover what blossomed. More often than not, it's a crop worth harvesting.

Of course, there are lessons in the setbacks as well, sometimes even more valuable. I've learned through hardship that progress is a fickle thing, not showing itself when you're expecting it. When that happens, it's easy to become discouraged or even lose hope. Don't.

Always believe that someday the stars will line up exactly the way you want them to. And even if they never do, the thrill that comes from touching those stars is only equaled by the personal satisfaction that comes from reaching for them.

♦♦♦

We had a record-breaking snowstorm this past winter. Back in my competitive days, I would have found a way to run in a storm like that. I'm not sure whether it was a durable body or a reckless spirit that compelled me to do so, but I lack both of those things now, so my only workout that day came in the form of heavy snow and a shovel.

When I was done, I stood on the back patio for a few moments admiring the scene. The snow was beautiful. There was peace in the muffled silence until I realized something was missing. There were no boot prints or sledding paths in the snow. My children have moved on.

It's funny how our day-to-day routines shelter us from a life that's constantly changing until something stops us for a moment so we can take an inventory. It's not like I didn't realize that they were getting older, but something in that moment made the fact more real.

I knew when they were born that my role as a father would be the most important of my life. And yet, there didn't seem to be any instructions to follow, so I've pretty much learned along the way. Making it even more difficult, there are no real ways to measure success.

Both of my children have grown to become good people; some would use that as a barometer, but they, not I, deserve the credit for that. Over the years, I've found that what I say to them has only a marginal effect. It has been their experiences, and their reactions to those experiences, that have largely shaped them.

What I've finally come to realize is that my highest purpose as a father can be described in rather simple terms - to set an example for my children to follow. Here is where running enters the story and where I have the opportunity to share something of value with you.

If you want your children to be strong, demonstrate strength. If you want them to be successful, illustrate the qualities that success requires. If you want them to be happy, show them that there is more to life than deadlines and responsibilities.

Running has allowed me to do all those things. As I've trained, overcome challenges and crossed finish lines, my children have watched me. As I've found joy and passion on my runs, they have noticed. In the process, they've learned more than they have from all the speeches, rules and punishments combined. It's not that those other things don't have an important place, but you can't guide your children with them if your own personal principles are misguided.

We all have a vision of what we'd like to become – a great athlete, a good parent, or simply a good person. Whatever your vision might be, the principles of running – things like discipline, resilience and consistency – will serve you well. And if you should ever need a little extra motivation to practice these, let it come from the eyes that are watching and following your lead.

◆◆◆

I knew every split needed to run a ten-mile race in 55:50. And, in case I forgot, they were written down with ink in the palm of my hand.

I was twenty-two, and I didn't have a coach or any real training plan. The only things I understood about running were these: I had a knack for it, and the hard work was paying off. Every race was an experience of discovery.

The warm August day was just beginning to cool as a small but talented field gathered at the starting line. The first mile of the out-and-back course was gradually uphill, but my excitement pulled me through that mile in 5:19. Two runners were keeping me company, and we continued to breeze through the second mile, passing that mark in 10:34.

I realized that I was the one pressing the pace, and backed off as the course began a three-mile climb towards the turnaround point. I was well ahead of my target and more than willing to bide my time until we started heading back home.

The other two runners seemed at my mercy; I relaxed, letting them linger on my shoulder. They hung there until we reached the turnaround in 27:53, two seconds faster than my goal pace.

It felt good to have the hardest part of the course behind me, and I accelerated on the downhill. Within a hundred meters, I was by myself. The runners still heading out watched me run by as mile six passed easily.

During the seventh and eighth miles, the road got quiet, and I relished the feeling of control. The final water station was at the eight-mile point, and I grabbed a cup and looked at my watch, passing the mark in 44:08. Even if I slowed considerably, I would reach my goal.

I could feel the fatigue growing during the ninth and tenth miles, but my momentum carried me as I made the final climb. I pushed through the downhill of the last mile and crossed the finish line in 55:05, glad it was over, but wishing the adrenalin high would last a little longer. The numbers in the palm of my hand were smeared in sweat, and I smiled as I wiped them away.

I'm almost embarrassed to say this, but I didn't understand how fortunate I was back then. I was blessed to be able to run away from competition and feel the unusual thrill of winning races. The bliss was almost blinding, and I would continue to run and race without any real plan or direction. Looking back now, I know I fell far short of my potential.

Most of us either fail to understand or fail to accept

an important truism of life – the promise of today is temporary. Before you know it, something you are lucky to have will be gone.

Fortunately, wisdom is mostly gained by making mistakes, and now I fully embrace the blessings in my life, most of which are far more important than running fast.

How about you? Do you see the possibilities in front of you? Are you embracing what you love? Whatever your answer, one thing is certain. Most things fade away in time, like ink pen from a sweaty palm.

Chapter 10

Tranquility

Serenely Quiet and Peaceful

Just as the sun touched the horizon, a young deer moved away from the others. Exploring the edge of the woods, she found acorns that had fallen through the night. She was getting her share before the squirrels started gathering.

A few miles away, I had just started my run: stiff legs were asking me to turn around; I ignored them, knowing they would stop complaining soon. Earlier, when the alarm had gone off, I wanted to keep sleeping. I had won that battle as well - two small victories.

It was a crisp morning. The world was colored with change and the air was new. I hadn't turned on the TV or the radio that morning. Nothing had spoiled the day, and it was perfect.

I remember moving along the trails, not paying much attention to my pace. You could say it was more of an exploration than a run. There was so much beauty that it was hard to take it all in. The smells of the earth reminded me of my high school years, when I ran around the corn fields and through the woods around the school.

There was no sound, except for my breath. It was almost like someone had hit the mute button on life. And in the slow rhythm of my breathing, the sights passed by like a parade, one striking picture after another.

Those runs are the best - effortless, with no thought of distance, just moving through the space around me. It was like I was a part of it all, even though I was miles from home in the middle of a place I had never been before.

I first saw her as I came around a turn. I stopped, and she looked up and stared. I know it wasn't long, but those few moments passed slowly as we both considered why we had crossed paths. Then she was gone, quickly moving back in the direction from which she had come, leaving fewer acorns for the squirrels to gather.

I stood there for a few more moments, wishing she had stayed a little longer. As I lingered, the sounds of the world returned with the breeze rustling the trees and the birds waking up.

My run was over before I wanted it to be, and I had to get my day started. There's always something that needs to be done. But the rest of my day was touched with a feeling that I was blessed. There was beauty in the world and I would see it again – soon.

It's funny how the running itself was never my motivation. That came from my competitive spirit and the desire to run fast. Now that my fastest days are well behind me, most of what I appreciate isn't about the races, but about the quiet runs.

I appreciate the peaceful feeling I find while everyone else is still in their beds and the freedom of being a part of something much bigger than myself. And, more than anything, I appreciate the paths that I cross, even if for the briefest of moments.

♦♦♦

It had been a difficult meeting, but I kept my emotions concealed as I walked to my office and sat down at the computer to check the latest news. The market was down again, and the politicians were sparring amongst themselves with little regard for honesty towards us. I looked at the running bag sitting in the corner with a sense of relief.

I ran straight to a familiar, grass trail. In the distance, I could hear traffic from the highway; people hurried toward the next thing on their schedule.

The rushing noise slowly faded away as I became aware of a different sound - birds singing to welcome me back. They darted around as if they were inviting me to join them in their game. Up ahead, a pair of geese sat on the path. Just before I reached them, they moved aside and fussed. I slowed down and fussed back, pretending they could understand, then laughed at myself. Sometimes I'm the only comedian I find entertaining.

The world turned silent after that, except for the rhythm of my breathing. I ran on autopilot, letting the path steer. There was a wide stream running full beside me and a lone deer watched from the other side. I wondered what she was thinking.

I reached the end of the trail and reluctantly turned around. After falling into a runner's trance on the way back, it surprised me when I realized the run was almost over, and I felt a strong urge to stop. It wasn't fatigue, but a desire to keep the world away for just a little longer. I didn't fight it.

I slowly walked along the path and saw the birds darting back and forth again. There were buds on trees and the grass was waking up. The path would look different soon.

I heard the sound before I saw him - a red-headed woodpecker - and I searched until I found him on the side of a tree. As I stood on the path, he danced from place to place trying to find the right spot, and I realized that I was way ahead of him. Like so many times before, running had led me to a perfect place.

I remember my first business trip to Chicago. Lonely and homesick, I ran down to the trail by Lake Michigan. Within moments, I was surrounded by hundreds of other runners, and the loneliness faded.

Running has brought me seclusion when I was overwhelmed and friends when I needed support. It's led me toward inspiration and away from discontent. It seems like when each run is over, I'm in a better place then I was when it began.

I guess I can't think of too many things much more important than that. After all, isn't that what each one of us is doing - searching for a better place?

I watched the woodpecker for a few more moments before starting to run back toward the office. In the distance, the sound of traffic began to rise.

♦♦♦

You've heard of the book The Loneliness of the Long Distance Runner. I've never read it, but its title creates an image that I've never really understood. Perhaps one of the most treasured aspects of being a runner is having time alone to think, to feel, and to sort things out.

I remember a run on a winter morning a long time ago. I drove out to the middle of nowhere to find a quiet trail to run away on. There was a dusting of snow on the ground, and there the world was a quiet place. As I began to run, only my footfalls broke the silence.

It seemed like even the animals stayed away as I wandered through the woods that morning, though the tracks in the snow showed they were there before me. The crisp air frosted my breath and, by this time, my breathing mixed with my footfalls to create a rhythm.

I ran by fallen trees, along streams and through pine trees. I ran over hills and through valleys. Off in the distance there was nothing more than what was right in front of me - miles and miles of solitude. I wasn't aware of speed - only movement. It was like I was daydreaming, watching the world around me but locked safely inside myself.

I ran until the weight of the world was gone. By that time, my car was miles away. It had started snowing, and the flakes made it feel like I was running in a snow globe. The peacefulness was overwhelming, and I had to stop for a while to take it all in.

Have you ever heard the sound of snowflakes landing in the forest? Have you ever felt as if the nearest person was a hundred miles away? Somehow, that day, those sounds and those feelings were exactly what I needed.

Running has always done that - given me what I need. When I was in high school I needed identity. Afterwards, I needed achievement. Some days, I've just needed a reason to be proud of myself. Running has always delivered.

I turned around an, followed my footprints, returning the same way I had come. I was a bit reluctant as I approached the end, not wanting the run to be over. I glanced back as I got into my car; then I left that place feeling a thousand times better than when I had arrived.

Perhaps some would call that loneliness, but I'm not one of them. I've journeyed alone thousands of miles along the roads and trails near my home. While people I've known have spent their time searching for the things they thought would make them happy, I've spent my running time searching for what seemed more valuable to me. And as I've run, the treasures weren't found in the world around me but inside myself.

Loneliness? I guess I've never felt that. Alone? Well, sometimes that's exactly what I need to be.

Chapter 11

Humility

A Lack of Fake Pride

I had just finished one of the best runs I had had in a long time. There was almost no pain from my stubborn injuries and my legs were smooth and free. It felt good to open up and run fast.

Whenever I have a run like that, my mind turns to competition. I start to think about my past success and dream about what might be possible if the injuries would loosen their hold on me.

My son, Paul, runs too, but he's never had the competitive nature of his old man. So far, he's been more than willing to accept whatever running has offered him.

I was still thinking about my encouraging run when I got the phone call. Paul was ill and on his way to the emergency room. Before I could come to terms with what was happening, we were en route to Johns Hopkins Hospital where Paul could be better cared for.

The days that followed were filled with uncomfortable waiting as the doctors tried to figure out just what was making Paul sick. In those days, running hardly crossed my mind. It was only in the relief of learning that Paul was going to be fine that I packed a running bag one morning as I prepared to head down to the hospital.

That afternoon, Paul was asleep when I went outside to run a few miles. It was a different kind of run; I'm not used to city noise and endless concrete. I passed hundreds of people but didn't find one kindred running spirit, though I searched several times as I jogged in place waiting for traffic to pass.

I ran the city blocks around the hospital several times before I began to relax, and by the time the run was over I felt a peaceful calm that I desperately needed.

I wiped the sweat from my face as I walked back inside. I moved through the hallways and towards my son, thinking about how blessed I've been to have him in my life.

Things were hectic when he was young, but he had a way of reminding me to appreciate simple joy. I remember the belly laugh that lured me to play and the innocent wonder that led me to slow down and explore beside him.

It seems a bit ironic that he's taught me so much about life. After all, I thought I was supposed to be the teacher in the relationship. And while I've tried to share whatever wisdom I have to offer, his lessons to me have been just as valuable, if not more so.

When I walked back into his hospital room, Paul was still sleeping. I stared for a few minutes and whispered a quiet thank you.

I know myself too well to think I'm ready to stop dreaming about running faster, but it's a dream that can't live forever. When I'm finally ready to let it go, I'll take an easy run and try to keep it all in perspective, and it will really help if Paul's there running beside me.

◆◆◆

A few times each year, the runners I coach through my running program gather in Gettysburg for a run. I was on the battlefield planning the route for our next running excursion there.

After I was finished, I was getting ready to take a run myself when my cell phone rang. It was my daughter, Katie, who attends Gettysburg College.

She told me she had just received an email from the college's President's office advising the students that there had been a fatal stabbing on campus. Though she wasn't in any danger, the email had been unsettling, and

I think it made her feel better knowing I was close by.

When we were done talking, I started my run. Running on the battlefield has always been peaceful for me, and I can never exactly resolve the irony that peace could be so easy to find in a place that had witnessed such violence.

Still, like every time before, within minutes I was immersed in the calm beauty of the place. I ran along Confederate Avenue, where Robert E. Lee's army gathered before the famous attacks that were launched from Seminary Ridge.

I ran past trees that had borne witness to the battle and by stone monuments that told the stories of men. I ran through fields where spring flowers were just starting to show themselves and by distant mountains that watched as I passed. In the final mile, I was running hard, alive with the energy that always finds me during my runs there.

That afternoon, Katie called again. Rumors about the stabbing were beginning to surface and they all seemed to involve Emily, a girl Katie knew from her freshman year at the college. While we were on the phone, the rumors were confirmed.

Katie told me that she remembered Emily as someone who had showed her kindness at a time when kindness

102

was something she desperately needed. As we talked, hundreds of others were sharing similar memories, each one about a giving, caring, passionate soul who left us too soon.

I wasn't very helpful in finding answers to the questions Katie had. Listening was all I could offer.

Later, my thoughts turned to the run that morning and the enduring irony about the peace I find on the battlefield at Gettysburg. In a way, life is built around that irony. Tragedy is all around us. The trick, perhaps, is to find our own peace in the midst of it.

Discovering a reason for Emily's death is impossible. Still, if we search, we might find meaning in her life. Life, after all, is always shorter than we expect it to be. Knowing that can help us realize the importance of the day we are living at this very moment. If Emily could somehow find her voice, I have a feeling she'd tell us something like that.

Maybe that's why I love my runs in Gettysburg. As I pass through humbling fields that remind me how real death is, I feel very much alive.

◆◆◆

After watching high school racing for dozens of years, I know I've forgotten more runners than I remember. Some, though, are unforgettable, like Rob Magin.

Rob was a tenacious competitor, usually leading the field beside teammate Joe Kershner. By the time he graduated in 1988, he had been named to several all-county and all-conference teams, but that's not what comes to my mind when I remember him.

Rob was quiet and refined. His high school coach referred to him as a "student of running." His hard work, combined with his intelligence, made him a feared competitor, and allowed him to continue his success at UMBC, where he earned many scholar-athlete honors and won a 10K conference title.

Rob and Joe Kershner stayed close during college. One summer, Rob had offered to take his younger sister to Hershey, Pennsylvania for a concert. He asked Joe to come along, and the two of them amused themselves for three hours in a half empty parking lot, passing the time with made-up games and conversation.

Rob eventually settled in Montgomery County, Maryland with his wife Jennifer. Their children, Mary Beth, Paul and Christine, now range in age from ten to two years. Between his devoted time with his family, and his dedicated work as an accountant for Marriott International, Rob managed to continue running and racing.

In 1994, he was named the Montgomery County Road Runners Club Runner of the Year, a title everyone understands he would have held continuously, had it not been for the rule that each runner can only win the award once. In the years since, he has run ninety-one local races, winning forty-eight and finishing second another twenty-one times.

In March of 2007, a stranger shared a seat with Rob, as they took a bus ride to the start of the Seneca Creek Greenway 50K trail race. The stranger was nervous, and Rob offered support and course advice. What he didn't share, and the man beside him only learned later, is that Rob was the defending champion, having won the race the previous three years. Rob's humility touched people.

On May 4, 2008, Rob ran the Hills of Cabin John 5K cross-country race. He finished second, never suspecting it was the last race he would run. Several weeks later, he was diagnosed with a malignant brain tumor. Afterward, I heard he had recovered, but never heard anything more, until earlier this month - when I learned he had passed away.

Running brings out the best in those who run, as it crafts discipline and fortitude. Every once in a while, though, a special runner passes through our lives who redefines running; a person who brings their own special character to the sport, and enhances an already virtuous avocation. Rob, as much as any runner I know, has done that.

It doesn't seem right, does it? How could such a good life be cut short? On the other hand, life is better measured by things other than time, and by such measures, Rob's life was long indeed.

Chapter 12

Joyfulness

Great Happiness

I sorted through my clothes but couldn't find the black socks. I made a note to stop at the store on my way to the church, and then I went outside to start my run.

It was a January morning in 1988. The cold air almost stunned me, and snow covered the ground from a storm just days before, but I needed a run to calm my nerves. It was going to be a big day.

It was early, and the streets of town were vacant. As I moved past the buildings, I could see my reflection in the windows from the corner of my eye, and I couldn't resist the urge to watch myself. It felt good to be running well again.

The year before had been difficult. In a blessed life, it's the one time I'd rather forget. As if the days weren't already hard enough, I had to face them without running because I was enduring a serious injury. Since the pavement was off limits, I found myself in the pool to maintain my fitness.

It was in the midst of all of this that I first met her. I remember the moment vividly. She introduced herself as I was walking to the locker room. We talked for a few moments and then each went our own way, but we said hello each time we saw each other after that. Before long, I was looking for her whenever I went to the club for a workout.

As I continued running through town that day, I saw her apartment in the distance. For a moment I considered stopping, but afraid she might still be sleeping, I ran past.

My pace quickened as I headed back home, and I realized the tempo would have been impossible just months before. Progress had been slow after the injury, but I was starting to set goals again. To a competitive distance runner, goals equal survival. The hard work is impossible without understanding what's at stake. And by this time, I was working hard for both of us. I wanted her to be proud of me.

When the run was over, I walked for a while before going back inside. I've always enjoyed the quiet of morning, and the peaceful feeling was going to stay with me for a long time. I wasn't likely to forget anything about this particular run.

I showered, shaved and then got dressed. I stared at the mirror for a few moments thinking how much I hated the tuxedo, but I knew she'd think I looked handsome. I stopped by the store for the black socks, and then went on to the church.

In the years between then and now, I've smiled at the irony many times. It was in the midst of heartache that I found my greatest love.

It seems somehow appropriate that it was running that led me in the right direction at a time when I didn't know where I was headed. Maybe you've noticed - running is the thread that holds most of the pieces of my life together. She holds all the rest.

◆◆◆

I stepped out onto my back deck just before heading up to bed. It was a perfect late summer evening, and I couldn't resist taking a moment to enjoy it. The locusts were calling out, telling me the gradual transition between summer and fall had begun. The cool air smelled exactly like it did when I was a boy, when I would play outside until the darkness made the ball nearly impossible to see. By this time in the evening, my mom would have called me inside.

I grew up outdoors. We played baseball in the summer and football in the winter, and we altered the rules based on whatever circumstances were presented. Two boys were enough to make two teams.

From the time I could walk until the time we moved away from my childhood home, I must have run a thousand miles in my own back yard. There was exhilaration in pulling the fresh air into my lungs and peace when I lay down in the grass. I can still remember watching the clouds pass by as we took breaks between games.

Having grown up playing sports, I fancied myself the athlete when I went to high school. I didn't understand that my small build was a hindrance until the basketball coach decided he didn't need a tiny point guard. After that, running itself became my game of choice. There were no size requirements for a distance runner.

From that point on, the roads and fields where I ran became my playground. As I grew older, running gave me relief from the daily pressures of life. Running was my exploration. It was my play.

Fatherhood changed things. It shifted my priorities. I gave up my focus on running in favor of things that were more important. I needed to be a dad without worrying about getting outside for a run. And so, play time came when life permitted, which wasn't all that often.

My son, Paul, is my second child. From the moment his personality began to show itself, there was a glow around him, as if his very soul resonated. Paul was filled with joy.

As he grew, I realized how blessed I was to have him. He explored the things around him in ways that led me to new discovery myself. His belly laugh lured me down onto the floor where he gave me something I had been missing more than I realized. For as long as I can remember now, I've looked forward to playing with Paul.

I was resisting it, but the locusts were making me face the truth - fall was coming again. It was going to be different this time because it was the fall that Paul began his senior year of high school. His passions were leading him in new directions.

It's sad to see him move on, even if I knew it was coming all along. I'm just glad that I have running, so I can feel the exhilaration of pulling fresh air into my hungry lungs, and so I still have something all of us need, and many fail to keep - play.

♦♦♦

The Baltimore Running Festival is growing. The event features a marathon, a marathon relay, a half-marathon, and a 5,000-meter race. In 2009, more than twenty-thousand runners participated. They came from forty-four countries and all fifty states to run, and I can hear the collective question coming from the minds of all the non-runners who read this – why?

It is a reasonable question. If you include both the male and female divisions of the races, there were only eight champions. Count the other runners who had enough talent and preparation to potentially win, and you could include no more than a hundred runners in the most elite category. So, the thrill of victory can't be the primary motivator.

Running is hard. It involves discomfort. In order to complete one of the races, participants had to train by running many miles, something the average person might not consider appealing.

Afterwards, the runners had little to show for their effort except for a commemorative shirt and a participant's medal. You really can't say that either of those things enhances a person's life.

And yet, they came on their own initiative, without coercion. They spent their own dollars on registration fees and travel. They used public bathrooms and port-a-pots that were not pleasant. They endured the anxiety of

112

waiting and pressed into the crowded starting areas. And then they ran a race. Why?

If you asked them directly, you would get a wide variety of responses. You would talk to doctors, lawyers, teachers and soldiers. You would hear from some who were retired and others who were unemployed. And, in the diversity of the stories you would find a common theme - something was missing from each life before running entered into it.

Understanding that leads me to a more important question. We lead lives of abundance. We have conveniences that our parents never dreamed about. There are programs and initiatives designed to provide for the basic needs of every individual, and yet there seems to be more discontent now than ever before. Why?

I'm certain that heated debate could stem from our attempt to find an answer, but since I'm a simple man, my thinking tends to be simple as well. You won't find anything profound in my conclusion, but here it is anyway.

The answer to both questions is the same. More food, bigger homes and better gadgets only touch the surface, and one basic human need runs deeper. We need to be fulfilled.

Perhaps you've been wondering yourself – how is it that life can be so full yet so empty as well? It's because fulfillment isn't found in things but in knowing that we can accomplish something significant on our own initiative. And on the streets of Baltimore, twenty-thousand people did just that.

Of course, you don't need running to find fulfillment, but you do need something similar. And if you're not sure what that is for you personally, it might be time to start searching.

The lake was as smooth as a sheet of glass except for a few ripples out near the middle, with fish playing near the surface. A turtle poked his head out of the water and then ducked back under as we ran past.

We were running easy and relaxed, soothed by the surroundings. The night before, we had planned on getting up early and we were glad we did. It was a beautiful morning. And best of all, I was running with my daughter again.

We had both taken a long break from running - each of us for different reasons. My reason was simple; chronic injuries made me understand that my only ally was rest.

Her reason was more complex; running itself had become complicated. After breaking into high-school distance running with huge success, it had later been difficult for her to live up to her own expectations. The harder she tried, the harder it seemed. Disappointment mounted and the pleasure was gone.

It was a challenging time for both of us, but we had each come to our own, similar conclusion: to hold on to something we loved, we had to let it go for a while.

There was some irony in knowing that we had both left and then come back to running at the same time. I hadn't even thought about that until she mentioned it one day. And suddenly, we were partners embarking on a journey to discover just what running would mean as we brought it back in to our lives.

We turned away from the lake and ran up to a gravel road that stayed near the water. Our run had found a rhythm, and the motion relaxed us. Tall trees gave us shade and created a tunnel as we passed through.

She talked about recent experiences, her plans and her dreams, and I remembered how running together had always given me the chance to glance into her life. I listened.

The run was over too soon, and afterwards we stretched together and talked just a little more. As I watched her, I found myself already looking forward to the next time she would join me for a run.

Yet, in some larger sense, I'm always running beside her, even while we're apart. I know every parent will understand when I say that my emotions are forever linked with hers. Sometimes, it feels like my heart beats in her chest. So, as she begins a new running journey, I find myself making one simple wish – let it bring her joy.

I know she has the same hope for me, and as we both run through the good days and the bad, we'll rely on each other for support and inspiration. She'll ask me lots of questions, and sometimes I'll be helpful.

And, as often as we can, we'll meet and run. We'll talk a bit about our challenges and successes, but none of that will matter very much, as together we find a rhythm and enjoy time with the best running buddy either one of us has ever had.

Chapter 13

Gratitude

Being Thankful

I'm sitting in my running room, a place in the house where I can do my writing and coaching work, and I'm looking at a small wooden box with an inscription on a brass plate entitled "Mil's Money." To most, it probably seems out of place amongst the running memorabilia, even with the medals draped around it.

"Mil" is short for Mildred, my grandmother. When she died in 1993, I offered to say a few words at her funeral. My gesture was declined. We have a big family, and it didn't seem fair to allow one of the grandchildren to speak without the others having the chance to do so.

On the day of the service, I took a run along a familiar back road, thinking about what I would say if I had had the opportunity. The winter chill, clinging to the early March air, was more aligned with my mood than the buds and birds that told of spring.

I came upon an old family cemetery and felt an urge to stop there. I walked along the edge reading the names and dates. Surely, some of them had been grandmothers. What words were spoken when they were laid to rest?

As I finished my run, I thought about some of my favorite memories of her, and that's when it came to me. My grandmother and I were connected in a way I hadn't considered before.

When I was growing up, my grandparents and my parents would get together regularly for a game of cards. I can remember going to the kitchen during their games and inquiring as to who was winning. Many times, it was my grandmother who answered, "It doesn't matter who's winning, Dave. We're just having fun." Her factitious tone couldn't mask her competitive nature. She didn't like to lose.

When I arrived for the funeral, my uncle asked if I would still be willing to speak, and I had the opportunity to share my thoughts after all. I told the story I just told you, and then a story about myself straining to win in the final meters of a race. My own competitive spirit, I told those gathered, was a gift from her.

In the days that followed, the wooden box was given to me by a friend of my grandmother who had been touched by my words. He had played cards with her on many occasions, and the box was something my grandfather had made for him to keep the quarters that were earned by the winner of each game. His box was so small, he told me, because seldom did he win.

118

I wish I had recognized her gift before she was gone. Without it, running could never have taken me so far. Still, I'm thankful now to understand that I, too, will pass something along. We all will, and for better or worse, it may live on for generations after we're gone. That's why what we acquire is trivial when compared to what we give away, and that's why a small wooden box will always hold a place of honor in my running room.

◆◆◆

I paced in front of the starting line knowing that I was about to run the most important race of my high school career. As I moved to the line, I looked at the runner in lane one, a reigning state champion. We settled onto the line, the gun fired and I was on his shoulder.

We were racing a mile, four laps around the track, on a warm, windless day in May. By the time we hit the backstretch, we had already separated ourselves from the rest of the field.

The first lap ended with the starter holding three fingers into the air, but it didn't matter how far we had to go. I was focused on staying just off the lead. I don't remember much about the middle laps except that I became aware that the entire stadium had stopped to watch. No one was throwing or jumping.

When we entered the final turn, I was still on his shoulder. By this time, he knew exactly what I planned to do, and he made his move earlier than I expected. He had pulled ahead by the time we came off the turn.

When I remember the final straight, I relive it in slow motion. I was wide open, straining to catch up. The roar as we passed in front of the crowd helped me maintain my sprint, and we were stride for stride with twenty yards to go. I felt it when he broke, and my momentum carried me across the line a half a stride ahead.

I lingered near the finish line congratulating my competitors, and then I moved toward the infield where I had changed into my racing flats and left a t-shirt behind. As I moved in front of the crowded stands, I heard a voice call out above the others, "Good job, Dave. Well done." It was the voice of my father.

We all need fans, people who stand up and cheer when we win and stand by us when we lose. Maybe I didn't really understand it then, but the most wonderful thing about that moment was finding the faces of my parents in the stands and sharing it with them.

Like most of us, I had to become a father myself to appreciate my own parents. Now I know how deep my feelings go. I've learned how much I'm willing to sacrifice for someone else. And, I've come to understand how much they sacrificed for me.

I can't fully explain the impact that running has had on my life since then. I could never be as productive, content, balanced or loved if not for running.

And yet, as I watch my parents live into old age, I finally understand that I would never have been as successful, in running or in life, without my greatest fans.

It's impossible to surrender the debt I owe except to return it to my own kids, and I've tried to do that. Still, I want my parents to know that they have fans, too. So today, let them hear a voice calling out over the dim roar of life - my voice saying "Good job, Mom and Dad. Well done."

We built an addition onto our house, and the largest space is an office, a quiet place for me to write and do my coaching work. I call my new place "the running room."

In the basement, there is a big green tub that holds my old running awards, pictures and newspaper clippings. You might think that I love going through that stuff, but if you want to know the truth, it's a mixed blessing.

Inside, there are mementos from some of my best moments - gold medals and finish line celebrations. Then, there are other things that might seem just as wonderful if you haven't lived the rest of the story.

There is this one bronze medal in the box. It's big and shiny with an impressive engraving of a runner, but it's not the medal I wanted. I had trained for months to win that particular race, but I lost my focus on race day. So, among all the best memories, there are things that remind me of times I could have done better.

Not long ago, I opened the tub and one by one, remembered the day that was connected to each item. On one side of me I placed those things that made me proud. On the other side, I put the ones that made me feel regretful. When I was finished, I gathered up all the disappointments and finally, after all these years, let them go.

In the days that followed I polished my proudest awards and framed my favorite pictures. There's one newspaper picture from my first high school cross-country season. I'm running at practice and staring at the camera with this goofy smile on my face. The floppy left arm will confirm that it's me.

I placed that picture at the doorway of my running room. Then, using the ledge that surrounds the room, I arranged everything until I was happy with the presentation. When I was done, I stood back and admired it all. For the first time in my life, I appreciated my entire running journey, with no conditions attached.

Don't misunderstand. I know the lost opportunities and poor performances are still inside me, but I'm not going to dwell on them anymore. Instead, I'll simply tuck them away for the times when I need inspiration to achieve, or for days when I need wisdom to avoid a mistake.

We all have a pile of stuff to sort through. Maybe yours is in a box in the basement, just like mine was. Maybe it's tucked away in some closet or hidden deep inside your heart. Take it out. Separate the disappointments. Feel them one last time, and then leave them behind you. You don't need to keep them anymore.

We know how fast time moves along, and yet we spend so much of it lingering in the past. We fool ourselves into thinking that we can somehow recapture a moment, a day, or a year that's gone forever.

We all need to find peace and feel hope, but those things are elusive, until you stop yourself from wondering what could have been and begin dreaming about what might be.

Notes

Notes

Notes